This Is Not a Skyscraper

Also by Dean Kostos

Poetry–

Rivering

Last Supper of the Senses

The Sentence That Ends with a Comma

Celestial Rust

Plays–

Box-Triptych

Choral Text–

Dialogue: Angel of Peace, Angel of War

Anthologies–

Pomegranate Seeds: An Anthology of Greek-American Poetry

Mama's Boy: Gay Men Write About Their Mothers

This Is Not a Skyscraper

Poems

Dean Kostos

Red Hen Press | *Pasadena, CA*

This Is Not a Skyscraper

Book layout by Danielle Verde
Front cover design by Michelle Olaya-Marquez

Library of Congress Cataloging-in-Publication Data
Kostos, Dean.
[Poems. Selections]
This is not a skyscraper / Dean Kostos.—First edition.
pages cm
ISBN 978-1-59709-416-0 (softcover)
I. Title.
PS3561.O8432A6 2015
811'.54—dc23

2014037132

The Los Angeles County Arts Commission, the National Endowment for the Arts, the Pasadena Arts & Culture Commission and the City of Pasadena Cultural Affairs Division, the Los Angeles Department of Cultural Affairs, the Dwight Stuart Youth Fund, Ahmanson Foundation, and Sony Pictures Entertainment partially support Red Hen Press.

First Edition
Published by Red Hen Press
www.redhen.org

Acknowledgments

2 Bridges Review, "Colossus of Rust," "*The Liver Is the Cock's Comb*," and "Processions"; *Alimentum*, "A Cannibal's Suicide"; *Apalachee Review*, "Mademoiselle Twisto" and "Madame Serpentina"; *Assaracus*, "Momix," "Blue Glow—Law & Order: SVU," "Luminous Barge," and "Amadou Diallo's Ghost Reminisces" (The latter poem won second place in Jot Speak's Poetry Competition [UK]); *Beneath the Heaven Trees: A Central Park Love Story*, "Hermaphrodite"; *Big City Lit*, "This Unexpected Clock," "This Man, His Many Almond Thoughts," and "Human Blockhead"; *Bloom*, "Memoir"; *The Good Men Project*, "No Elegies for Porn Stars"; *Live Mag*, "Rain Seen from the Gym" and "Green Torch (Song)"; *Mediterranean Poetry* (Sweden), "The Naked Man," "The Etruscan Chariot," and "Bronze"; *Memoir Journal*, "*Prosopo* Means Face, Mask, Person: A Memory Album of My Mother, Sofia" and "1946"; *OCHO 22*, "At the Barber's," subsequently included in the anthology *Pears, Prose & Poetry*, received a Pushcart Prize nomination; *Rabbit Ears: TV Poems*, "New York Apocalypse," and "Master of the Bally—Scott Baker"; *Red Rock Review*, "Angelica," "Electra," "Nick Knack," "Sword Swallower (AKA Heather Holliday)," *The Same*, "Mana-Hata," "Bryant Park," "Friend, Almost Empty Café," "The Yacht Club," and "Algebraic Grace, 4 a.m."; *Sierra Nevada Review*, "Insomniac Neighbor"; *Spoon River Poetry Review*, "Scorpion Cowboy"; *St. Peter's B-list: Contemporary Poems Inspired by the Saints* (anthology), "Astoria"; *Talisman*, "Yolks" and "Flights"; *Taos Journal of Poetry & Art*, "Turkish Man with Cinnamon Eyes"; *Token Entry—New York City Subway Poems*, "Evidence that Leonard Bernstein Took New York City Subways" and "Subway Silk" (the latter poem, translated into short a film by Jill Clark, was screened in Tribeca and at the San Francisco Indiefest); *The Tusculum Review*, "Sub Rosa" and "Feeding History," published as "Eating History"; and *Voices of Hellenism Literary Journal*, "Astoria," "Bronze," and "The Naked Man."

With great pleasure, I thank Joel Allegretti, Star Black, Philip F. Clark, Mark E. Cull, Mark Doty, Kate Gale, Veronica Golos, Rachel Hadas, Richard Howard, Lynn McGee, Martin Mitchell, Karen Neuberg, Sharon Olinka, Molly Peacock, Carl Rosenstock, Nicholas Samaras, John Yau, and Michael T. Young, who have long believed in my work and encouraged me.

For My Mother, Sofia S. Kostos

Contents

One

Two

Three

Four

One

Amadou Diallo's Ghost Reminisces

An unarmed West African immigrant with no criminal record was killed on February 4, 1999 by four New York City police officers who fired 41 shots at him in the doorway of his Bronx apartment building.
—The New York Times

Ice cream tasted like America.
I bought a pint that night, caramel flecked
with almonds.   Celebration!
Sold more than my quota of gloves, scarves

& key chains. Saving for college. Savoring
spoonfuls, I ambled back to Wheeler Avenue,
back to the vestibule—
a bulb the only light,

bald eye.   Voices
pounced from darkness:
"Police—hold it. Stay there."
But they wore jackets & jeans. I fumbled

with keys, couldn't—
"Turn around. Keep your hands
where we can see them," they snarled.
                                   Shouts from every angle—

a hive of voices.
I couldn't think, couldn't act
fast enough—dropped
my keys, the ice cream.

"Here—my hands!"   I thrust them up
to the crescent moon,
my palms' pages waiting
to be inscribed.

"Yeah, that's him! Kid, show us I.D."
As I jammed hand into pocket
to grab my wallet, I looked down, saw
ice cream oozing from crushed cardboard.

"Gun—he's got a gun!" a cop growled.
Their voices became one
voice, their mouths the muzzles
of guns.   Metallic words bit

into me—one after one—
gashes—one after one—leaden flies
swarming, tearing my flesh.
What had I done? I tried

to ask, but fell . . .   couldn't fall far
enough, couldn't be slaughtered fast
enough, sharp metal
pumping into me, blood

sluicing pavement cracks,
the slivered moon reflected
in crimson. Bullets drilled
until I closed my lids:

saw myself float toward the vestibule, saw
myself slip through its closed door,
my forty-one eyes
                                                  gleaming.

Sub Rosa

On Thursday, November 11, 1999, Parks Department patrolmen found two large cow tongues nailed to an oak tree in Bronx Park near Kazimiroff Boulevard, each with a padlock clipped through a hole at the end of the tongue. "It appears that they are encouraging someone to be silent," said city Parks Commissioner Henry Stern.

—The Daily News

The news camera zooms close-up:
    two cow tongues crucified

to an oak. The salmon-colored scrolls
    loll, pierced at tips with padlocks,

some sub-rosa deed never
    spoken, never unlocked by tongue

—bovine *or* human. For whom
    is this pronunciamento meant?

Why not post the portent
    on an estate, where a gardener

with one filmy, gray eye & yellowed
    nails could find the quotation marks

surrounding a gasp?
    Instead, before joggers with headphones,

nannies with strollers, & bonds analysts
        with Shar-Peis, the tongues

slacken with padlock weight—
        blood, moo, & mute

secret drained through night's
        oh's.

Insomniac Neighbor

Our ritual of distance devours voices.

Blue heads float

in black, pre-dawn

air: your TV through a window

across the street—box

within a box. All else

disappears. Through branches'

accusatory wag, I eye

the watery faces:

to speak, they chew.

Now the blue heads

drift from tele-

vision—poisonous balloons

released by you.

You've Been Here Before

Yes, there were children clamoring
under artificial shade, selling invisible towers
to tourists, but there were also bicyclists
with enameled eggshells on their heads,
calling, "Watch out!"
I was not beneath buttonwood shade
when men with springy necks assembled
to assess my worth in dimming light.
I was the "ocean" setting on the white-noise
machine that sounded like traffic.
And the fleshy bicyclists
in sky-blue velour weren't really angry
after all. They were just paid to look that way
by the Department of Commodities.

New York Apocalypse

as seen on TV, sound off

Flickering into history's wind—
a banner embroidered with threadbare names.
Wearing a necklace of soaked tissues,
a woman wipes away her face.

The banner embroidered with threadbare names
dances like a ghost
wiping away her face.
A policeman's white horse is real, but the rider

glances like a ghost.
Men in black balmacaans detonate themselves.
The policeman's red horse is real, but the rider
bathes in a mirage.

Men in black balmacaans detonate themselves.
A child listens to helicopters' sputtering.
Bathing in a mirage,
a banker turns his back.

A child listens for helicopters, stuttering.
Wearing a pall of soaked tissues,
a banker turns his back
& flickers into history's wind.

Feeding History

as seen on TV, sound off

1963

A man in a black hat
is a fist, ushering an assassin
into a car. Blurred scurry:

Eadweard Muybridge's black &
white. Time frames are tall windows.

The assassin opens one, curves
his neck into the future, aims
the Mannlicher-Carcano.

1993

Behind a hospital curtain, a man
& woman drink each other's voices.
In Gotham fluorescence, a bomb-

pocked patient
arrives: mute eyes, ragged skull.

Orderlies suture
him to a mattress with black
script. A mirror devours his head.

2001

His neck is assumption,
her cheek acknowledgment.
His chin is suggestion, her kiss

a chevron. He deciphers
shadows scrawling across a glass tower.

She breathes words into the mouth
of a cell phone, feeds
herself to a window.

Blue Glow—*Law & Order: SVU*

First, learn to say "vic" & "perp" as you shuffle toward
another crime scene: a street
filled with dumpsters & cross-dressing hookers. Graffiti
advertises gangs like products. A monosyllabic swagger
proves detectives Benson & Stabler fearless. Wound
tight, they reveal no theory about the man's "slaughter."

But they're still not sure if it was murder or manslaughter.
Back at headquarters, the detectives lean toward
the glass wall where they affix a forensic collage: wound
with tape & photos of the corpse & street.
As neon leaks from the snapshots, Fin swaggers
to his desk & reads a misspelled letter scribbled in graphite.

From the perp? Benson & Stabler graffiti
the glass wall: arrows, circles, underlines. Manslaughter
(or worse?) hovers like a corpse's portrait by Duchamp. Swaggering
into the office, the DA is peeved. He rifles through untoward
photos, unable to find the one taken on Little West Twelfth Street.
The forensic pathologist bursts into the room, "The wound

wasn't the cause of death. The vic was mummified alive, wound
with gauze . . . suffocated!" A handwriting specialist claims graffiti
is a signature—no two alike. The street
must contain the clues. So far, the perp of the man's slaughter
eludes capture. As the janitor's broom scuffles toward
their desks, Benson, Stabler, & Fin finally stagger

home. A text message: *Meet me at the abandoned brownstone.* Staggering,
Stabler pries the door: no lights. Biblical scripture wound
like webs: *Thou shalt, thou shalt . . .* Two words
never seemed so ominous. Illegible graffiti
is carved into a banister like a tattoo on a slaughtered
man's arm. What did this Wall Street

broker get himself into? As Benson proceeds, she finds a dead street-
walker stuffed in a refrigerator. Stunned, she staggers
back, stumbling on an altar of candles, wax bleeding. Not manslaughter—
homicide. Even though they've found the vic's wounds,
there are no blood stains. But each crime announces itself like graffiti.
Questions of *who* & *where* shuttle toward

Manhattan streets, wound like phrenic nerves. Following
the graffiti, Stabler staggers toward the kitchen & sprays Luminol.
The blue glow enlivens blood's trace, the sapient stain: man's laughter.

Bryant Park

In the tunnel beneath Bryant Park, quotations from Ovid, James Joyce, Carl Jung, and others are embedded in mosaic.

Descending into Ovidian fluorescence,
        into Joycean rhetoric, I lose

myself in syntax, corridors.
        Dusty veins tangle

into maps, histories. I climb stairs
        to find what isn't contained

by borders. Sky unpeels itself from color—
        blue vibrates between

branches. Twigs spell something inscrutable
        in Linear B.

Who can decipher the past? Who stands
        behind its indelible writ?

Havened by a halved cupola, William Cullen Bryant
        pries a page of his bronze

New York Post: abolition affirmed,
    advertisers bleeding ink.

The approaching roar
    of Civil War.

New York Bleeds

through its
music: jazz from
saxophones, seeping up
like slow, dark oil from the depths of
subways

Subway Silk

Dozing
lightly on the
express train from Ninety-
Sixth to Seventy-Second Street,
I hear

a cool
whispering &
feel my fingertips rush
over silk, then feel hot breath trill
over

my limbs,
abdomen, chest,
eyelids, until I am
awakened by the conductor
singing

the name
of my station.
And then I see the source
of the chafe: the rubbing of two
nylon

backpacks.
Two people: one
a woman, one a man—
both unaware their backpacks are
touching.

Evidence That Leonard Bernstein Took New York City Subways

As the train pulls away,

it wails the first three notes

of "Somewhere": *There's a place . . .*

but never finishes the phrase,

syntactical or musical, never

keens *for us,* as if the train

—knowing it will never cease

its peregrinations,

never find a station

to rest in, until breaking

down, retired to a yard—

still yearns

to belong.

Flights

When I climb down the fire escape.
snow scalds my eyelids.
The lottery seller's wife molts white feathers,
so I call out her name scribbled in my notebook.

When I climb down the pier's pilings,
a seagull's cry halves my brain.
A man who carves amulets has nowhere
to sleep, so I sing him a *fado* from a Portuguese book.

When I climb down subway stairs,
I trample a carpet of unread letters,
light a candle in a blacked-out corridor,
& free an engraved starling from a chapbook.

When I climb Payson Avenue to the Cloisters,
blistered angels wait for me to sell them time—
forsythia shriveling at their footsteps.
I chant their names, illuminated in incunabula.

When I rove Forty-Fourth Street, my shadow
writhes from the asphalt.
As his questions tangle with those of ghosts,
I watch them all catch fire—wings like opened books.

Algebraic Grace, 4 a.m.

I
slouch
silent
as milk, pass
an ash tree, pinions
fanning. A brick wall imprinted
with shadows of a pigeon heavening from granite

eaves.
The
diseased
wings scissor.
I scrape at awe, frail
vertigo. A skyscraper, sleeked
into epic, rises from asymmetric beams.

The Yacht Club

37 West Forty-Fourth Street

Stone waves spill from a Dutch galleon, flowing
from window to window.

Each column devises
a soaring arch as it rises

into a façade. In January
light, the wooden pergola unfolds windy

sails, ragged wraiths. Nothing can solidify
a liquescent building. No colonnade can codify

this surge toward mind's ocean:
An empress peers from a window in the galleon.

Cornices surround the emperor as she tells him
they'll sail to a lost forest of columns.

While these sovereigns never
existed—more than the shadow of a feather—

convex faces smudge the pane. Their unknown
mouths gape, sighs hardening into stone:

breaths exhaled centuries ago—alive, all
tumbling into wind. Destination: the arrival.

Con Edison Building

Carved from
moon, this building
looms, its clock encircled
by ceremonial urns, flames
sprouting.

Madison Square Park

Echo, by Jaume Plensa, is a 44-foot-tall sculpture.
It occupied the main lawn from May to August 2011.

Guarding the entrance, William Seward crosses
        oxidized legs. His preposterous head

revolts against his body
        as the lawn goes purple.

A woman dressed
        in frayed ghosts leads children

by threads to see a girl's four-story
        head: eyes closed, mouth

an anemone. The decapitated
        girl repeats her name: *Echo* . . . I go . . .

At the foot of Metropolitan Life,
        a white-haired guitarist snips

electric nerves connected to the past, music
        reverberating . . . berating . . .

A window opens onto colonies
        of others. Behind each, an unanswered

question . . . quest one . . .
        Inside a shuttered window,

the memory of a girl—nothing
        remaining but her voice.

Two

Mana-Hata

As a boy, I named
myself Red Feather & dug
for arrowheads—New

Jersey soil entombed
history. I scarified
the earth with a twig:

Lenni-Lenape,
Munsee, Powhatan. Today,
tutelary wraiths

spark from concrete like
radioactivity.
Manhattan bares its

beams, its razed columns,
corbels—its want. Gray feathers
float above Wall Street.

The Stock Exchange sounds
its plangent bell: *There is no*
beginning to return to.

To a Corbel

Saint Ignatius Loyola Church, East Eighty-Fourth Street

The word
is a crow's beak.
Form whorls into sight, a
wave implied in mute stone. Marvel
the deed:

masons
hewed volutes where
stability did not
demand them. Are we crows circling,
our beaks

stuffing
craws? Or are we,
because our calendars
are fixed, fixated on wanting
to last:

a wave
coiling from time's
sea, roiling from mason,
painter, or poet who gleaned the
depths of

fear &
reformed them, to
chisel into sandstone's
implacable monument: "I
was here."

In Union Square

Stage hands erect stone
walls. Aimed at vacant arches,
floodlights flank the gilt
proscenium—each arch will
encase a vignette, spoken

by mouths bending wind
into (inspire!) the playwright's
words. Each spire of lights
sits on a tripod swathed in
red. Banners flounce & flame from

doorways, soon to be
unlocked. A Buddha waits in
the wings. He declared
one dies neither too early
nor too late: exits, entries

porous with portals
of human want. Gautama
sits in lotus pose,
his bun adorned with snail-shell
curls. Five stage hands haul pylons,

the stage becoming
sea. The unconscious seeps—a
liquid realm—ocean-
womb of creativity,
amniotic void. Is that

why this polychrome
Buddha seems so amused, a
smile sliding across
his lips? If we navigate
the gulf between knowing &

being—dying to
the raucous currents of self—
can we ignite mind's
lotus, an unseen mouth like
an actor's yet to perform?

Processions

The Gates, *an installation in Central Park by*
Christo & Jeanne-Claude, February 2005

Flaming ghosts slant through branches.
    Immaterial material
        shrouds a snowy graveyard. Are we
            mourners or mourned?

Samurai banners whip through landscape.
    Shinto wraiths sing
        a ginger-colored god. Where
            goes his shapeshifting form?

A Bulgarian march drones from the carousel.
    Cavalcade from Tartar encampments,
        guidons flickering by campfires.
            Where have the soldiers trudged?

Art as elegy: steel bones, cloth flesh.
    People in mold-colored coats step through fire,
        arrive at Seurat's *Grande Jatte.*
            Transported? Transmuted?

Disembodied voices scatter
    like powdery snow. Branches stiffen
        into characters, imprint saffron robes:
            Feed yourself to Buddhist flames.

Yolks

You told me
I want to break yolks of lava with you

but the only eruption you provoked
was an artificial sun

emblazoned with the numerals
ticking inside you

You repeated them each hour
to statisticians

You told me we are rioters
against the contract between name & named

but when Central Park poison ivy
tangled over our mouths

a skein of script
rewrote our desires before we spoke them

You told me you'd rewrite us in cursive
set to the discordant music of the calliope

to the vertiginous yellows & reds
of lullabies & curses

Carousel

Central Park

Baroque horses carve summer wind.
If they chased & fled themselves
—revolutions following a fixed center—
would hungers grow?

Chasing & fleeing themselves,
the beasts' bare cannibalistic muzzles. Teeth gleam.
Wooden hungers grow.
Children's screams belt into centrifugal air.

Cannibalistic muzzles flare, teeth gleaming.
Small hands grasp the manes.
Children's screams melt into centrifugal air,
decades passing with each rotation.

Watching time erode, children gasp. The manes
flare above saddles from which riders never leave.
Decades pass with each rotation.
flame-&-leaf patterns twist with thorns

on saddles from which riders never leave.
Muscular necks arch & swallow
flame-&-leaf patterns, entwined with thorns.
Hurdy-gurdy plays, "Ob-La-Di."

Muscular necks arc & swallow,
revolutions following a fixed center.
Hurdy-gurdy plays, "Ob-La-Da."
Baroque horses carve autumn wind.

Hermaphrodite

Dancers, tumblers that leap like lambs,
Agile as arrows, like shots from a cannon,
Throats tinkling, clear as bells on rams,
Will you leave him here, your poor old Villon?
—François Villon, translated by A. S. Kline.

Reading
François Villon
by Bethesda Fountain,
I hear wails, bells, drums. Shadows hiss
from the

shriek of
a berdache. This
man(?) saws a violin,
chants rumbas. Kohled eyes. Fount of dread-
locks. All

(s)he wears
is a golden
breechcloth, veiling more fore
than aft, secret of the gender(s)
untold.

But this
body appears
male: coppery muscles.
Ankles sport hives of bells, bangles.
Yma

Sumac
(reborn!) lights a
fire: ancient oblation.
Shrill barks incite the crowd: bills float
into

an urn.
Incense-ghosts rise
from the shrine. A yin-yang
symbol perched above a bronze book:
HERMA.

Coney Island Sideshow

NICK KNACK

His gender is as ambiguous
as her race. He (she?) seems
as confused as we are by the theme.
But Nick's choice isn't arduous
at all. While the curious gawk,
(s)he stares at a shelf of curios: objects
coffined in cases. First, Nick inspects
them: a deformed Abraham Lincoln, a chalk-
pale wedding-cake couple,
a garter snake, even a teacup. One
by one, (s)he picks them off the shelf.
Like a frog on its supple
pad, flicking a fly with its sticky tongue,
Nick gobbles down each one—*humph!*

SWORD SWALLOWER (AKA HEATHER HOLLIDAY)

Her emblem: a heart laced like a corset, only
with knives. How Tarot, with its suit of swords:
numina slashing through matter. She

bends into her garden of blades
as if to suck them down. She begins to say, "I'll . . ."
& then ingurgitates her destiny. Now, she braids

camellias into her red curls, to beguile
those in the audience who
haven't been paying attention. While,

for the rest of us, this talent is a mere preview
of another. High-heeled, with ashen
skin, she stomps stage left. Wearing torn peek-a-boo

lingerie, she collapses (from passion?)
into a heart-shaped couch, swords stabbing every
which way—a pain cushion.

SCORPION COWBOY

How does he tend to the body's needs?
Clunk! His pincers thud like sand-filled shoes.
Making his mother's body bleed

when he was a boy, he swore he'd
mask his thalidomide shame like a bruise.
Unable to tend to his body's needs,

surgeons vainly tried to debride
but had to amputate. Scorpions ooze
venom but do not bleed.

His purple pincers are parentheses. Read
the clause: to love is to lose.
So he wrangled his heart's needs,

shunning daylight, affirming this creed:
live on a stage of thorns & desert views.
Never planting his body's seed,

he's middle-aged now. Even if he did succeed,
he's worn self-loathing like a noose.
How does he tend to his body's needs
without making his body bleed?

HUMAN BLOCKHEAD

Mustachioed Mr. H. Blockhead
sports a bowler hat. He believes
in being dapper: white striped shirt (no blood bled)
& garters worn like waists on voluminous sleeves.
Hammer in one hand, nails in the other,
is he a carpenter? Is he building a boat to sail
or a casket, plank-by-plank? Neither:
he slams nail after bloodless nail
up his nose. Couldn't this be fatal?
As if replacing something
vital he lacks, he inhales the metal
& is healed! Or is he killing
his own fear of death, delighting in audience
gasps? Some people flee. Pen to paper, I wince.

ANGELICA

Forget metaphor. Her tattooed face
is zebra. The ink wrinkles & sags.
Patterns layer until patterns erase

themselves: her black-white markings are zigzags.
Her crow-wing curve of hair
spans her shoulders like a swag.

Spewing balloons—prayers
of fire—she looks at us adoringly & growls,
"It *is* amazing, isn't it?" Unable to share

in her delight, we're mute & recoil.
Now the flames she exhales
leap out in zebra stripes. A gargoyle

fulfilling its function—to countervail—
she frightens the frightening. She prevails.

MADEMOISELLE TWISTO

Cubism is alive! Just look
at her two cats. They know
about alienated affections—calico
derangements, feline femurs flexed, tails hooked.

The legs of Madame's crooked
throne are octopus Art Deco.
In fishnet stockings, *her* legs torque
before a photograph of her French beau,

Fernandel. Because Mademoiselle misses Paris,
she lights up a Gauloise. As if starting to melt,
it droops from her magenta lips. She's both artiste

& her own model. In a boneless act of self-service,
she wraps her legs around her neck like a pelt
skinned from some endangered beast.

MADAME SERPENTINA

Can you hear the papyrus rustling together
as the moon rises—a dirty nickel, torn
from blue-cellophane sky? Whether

the snake is real or sewn is immaterial; it's worn
with Hollywood élan. In this scene,
Madame's glossy legs emerge—unadorned—

from a starlet's gown of red bengaline,
distracting our eyes from hips & bosom
so padded they're preposterous. Serpentine?

As the tarnished moon sinks, this lissome
viper slinks from her leather
skin—no milk, no sweat, no venom.

ELECTRA

Despite Hellenic moniker & matricide,
Electra, too, is Cubism's bride:

her fractured décor, her face
flashing sides: one a smile, one a grimace.

Notice her bloody manicure
& how her talons' curvature

zaps currents like curses to the past.
(A congress of ghosts can attest!)

Her voltage zigzags through the atmosphere,
elevating her like a Varanasi fakir.

As she rises up on serpents (a living necklace),
their shock-therapy tongues hiss, "Yes."

MASTER OF THE BALLY—SCOTT BAKER

Watch this master of ceremonies anointing
the air. A cruciform man—part
scarecrow, part weathervane—he starts
tilting & turning, as if pointing

with no aim at all. He's more seedy
than debonair with his warts, top hat & tails.
After his cane taps on tattooed boxes & bales,
they snap open—greedy

as shark gullets. Each touch mangles
some image of the freaks
we've seen. Bastard-amber lights vibrate

as a banner with all eight names tangles.
When the curtain cascades down with a shriek,
the floor shakes under its weight.

Momix

The Joyce Dance Theater

Torsos turn into faces, snarl
into horizons. While mountains emerge
from scrim-chasms, flashing
strobe lights transform spandex

into horizons. While mountains emerge,
voices chant from the pit
& black lights deform spandex
beasts. Their claws hook

voices, ranting from the pit.
They braid & bellow with syncopated
beats. Their awe unhooks
moments exploding above the audience.

Braiding & bellowing with syncopated
cellos, drums,
moments explode before the audience!
As the dancers dissolve into waves,

cellos & drums
flash from chasm-scrims.
Dissolving into waves, dancers'
torsos turn into faces, snarling.

Broadway

In a plaintive state of Sondheim's
        myriad mind, the audience

drowns. Soaked in darkness
        & bastard-amber

light, shadows melt
        into sung phantoms. *Sprechgesang*

imprints dark air, consonants
        carving vowels from a wound.

Green Torch (Song)

A Brooklyn oak in early May, I ache
        from colors singing through my veins.

Centuries have darkened, voices of the dead
        nattering, congealed

into sap. I have hardened—
        obsession spiraling from my rings:

becomingbecome . . . I want
        what exceeds my reach,

limbs scything distance:
        swatches blue & blue.

August: dust culls in leaves' nervure.
        Greens brown.

October ignites eyes: I churn,
        burn my colors out.

Wind & rain rinse me bald,
        my leaves choking gutters.

Hands stab pewter air with umbrellas,
        sky bleeding sky.

January: standing black
        against Brueghel snow,

I am indecipherable.
        Neither notion, notation

nor dark guitar, I am
        unstrung. Unsung.

Three

At the Barber's

I wait for Zoya—Russian for Zoë—I wait for life.
Every time I arrive, her hair's a different shade of marigold:
trumpet, egg yolk, cognac. She's been my barber
for years. Her chair's at the end

of the room, near hooks where jackets & sweaters
hang. Seated in her swiveling throne, I watch other patrons
in the mirror without turning my head, simply gazing
at reflections, & reflections of reflections.

I observe the dark-haired, young barber,
his chair next to Zoya's. Although he's also Russian, he speaks
English without an accent. His tea-colored
eyes are large, his lips a cursive lowercase "m."

His nostrils seem to have been shaped by pressing
an index finger into wet clay. Covered
with silky, black hair, his arms are "in velvet"—said of stags'
antlers when spring scents the air with musk.

It's been a long winter, & I'm here to be sheared
in anticipation of spring. As Zoya artfully clips & trims, I look
in the mirror & notice a man in his mid-thirties easing
into the adjacent chair. He's noticed me

noticing him, yet won't return
my stare, as if not to admit *I know who we are.*
Will he get his goatee trimmed? Is it dyed? Several shades
darker than the hair on his head. His features are rounded,

solid. He engages the barber in male banter—
artificial, learned, scripted—to fit in, to entice.
And it works. The two shift from politics
to weather, the customer closing

his eyes as the barber glides the electric razor
over the back of his head. His hair seems to crumble, falling
away like steel shavings to a magnet. While Zoya
meticulously snips short hair around my ears, I glance

into the mirror to watch the man who won't acknowledge me.
He's murmuring something as the barber lathers
the back of his neck. With tongs, the barber fishes into a jar
of blue disinfectant, retrieving a straight razor,

erasing foam & hair from newly revealed
flesh. The customer's eyes are closed.
(I can't look away!) The barber
massages the smooth skin of the man's neck

with lilac-scented astringent. I imagine the barber bending
down, planting a kiss, then pivoting
the chair, & pressing his lips to the man's mouth.
But realizing the cut-&-shave ritual

has ended, the client opens his eyes
& resumes the formality of feigned conversation.
Cape removed, he regards himself in the mirror,
thanks the barber, & dissolves

into brisk March air. Having tamed my hair, Zoya
wields a hand-mirror like a priestess, exposing
the back of my neck—
place I can't see for myself.

Memoir

These are the hours & those
the discarded papers.

This is the park & that the elm
from which we swung. This is a photograph

with its smeared halo. This is your stubble,
this your chewed nail.

These are the tongues of flowers—
mispronounced words

for defeat. This is your deleted chapter.
Those are trains with embered numbers

& this is subway wind.
Yes, this is the tunnel

& its vanishing point
no one ever reaches.

Phobia Canzone

Space expands, air whorling into
a vacuum. Your face clenches as you turn
into a barricade, stiffening your body to
contain chaos. But this Phobia is too
voracious. Inside a giant's cast-
iron death mask, you're trapped. It clamps onto
your life, announces its edict: *to*
never enter large, enclosed spaces. You try over
& over to conquer it, but end up over-
come by shame. *Give in to*
it, don't fight it, you reason, casting
a cooler light on your rank self—lowliest caste.

Sneak back into the world, Outcast.
Act as if nothing happened, continue to
perform work, perform . . . cast
in the role of "Capable & Organized," till Phobia casts
its thorny cloak around you, turning
you into one who avoids (no, is *cast*
out of) theaters, museums, airports, casting
shadowy wings over your apartment, prison cell.
Is Phobia genetic, a warped marker in your DNA cells,
the original, pristine ones cast
aside, now lacking a chromosome, compensated over
generations? Was your grandmother's tic an attempt to over-

throw the conquest of loss? Did *her* ancestors blench, over-
run by invading hordes? Hooves' tattoo? Cast
them out. But unboundaried space over-
whelms you as you lunge into an overly
large space, say, Grand Central Station. *Too*
dangerous—you'll be killed! Although this makes no sense, overtly
illogical thoughts trounce you. When the episode is over,
you're grateful to return
to your apartment—its walls a nest—until it's your turn
to enter another large, enclosed space, where, over-
strung by the need to flee, every cell
in you shrills, *Don't embarrass yourself.*

You run to appear rushing. Sell
that to passersby—pretend—this will be over
when you finally get outside. Cell
phone talkers & texters see your sweaty daze, your cel-
lular liquefaction running past their downcast
eyes. Nauseous, you hate yourself
& abandon the dream of altering your brain's cells
to welcome large spaces as serene. To
arrive at that state, you'd have to
halve yourself, tear skin, a cel-
lophane of perception & turn
into a man at ease with the world, knowing his turn

will come to turn
off the glare radiating from his flayed self,
his boy-self who never turns
away from this plea: *Turn*
into a wreath of arms. Soon the calm is over.
Hungry Phobia turns
against you, hunts you, turns
skyscrapers into jaws, your thoughts cast
into pools of bile. Fluorescence casts
a green tinge to your skin, your fear turned
inside out, no longer secondary of two:
equal. You admit defeat to

build a space for Phobia & live beside it, to
welcome it as a companion: actor cast
by you to perform your act of being overly
controlled. Meanwhile, inside each cell
hums a rapacious gullet, awaiting its turn.

Fear

crouches on the fire escape, taunting, "I
was you before you

were born." Opening locked windows, Fear stinks
of calf's liver burnt

on a black skillet. Its shirt & trousers—
color of yellowed

bruises. The room dims as Fear coos, "I am
you." Dust scatters on

books & letters. Fear scratches into cracked
linoleum, roaches

skittering. Scarified words: threats unread.
Fear inhales phonemes

as you speak them. Although it turns away,
it reforms itself.

In sticky dust beneath your bed, it spells,
I'll always be you.

The Art of Near & Far

I've been eating bones
          delicate from baking

year after year. They were
          my former selves.

Phantom wings encircle.
          A blue jay's rusty screech

admonishes,
          "Can't."

I decant lost decades
          through subway grates, await

alchemic renewal, transmute
          the inability to love

into love. I pour the cup.
          I spill it.

Friend, Almost Empty Café

Closing the door on winter wind,
we order chocolate mud pie & caffé macchiato. Its mist
dissolves as you discuss your musical
gift & training. From your mouth,
"But I didn't make the right friends . . ." spirals.
The storm batters plastic bags

into trees' claws. A flock of bags
snags onto the branches, buffeted by wind.
You detail betrayals: narratives spiral
through uneventful glories, missed
chances, stifled potential, "Like a hand over my mouth.
Now, all I have is my love of teaching music."

I say, "The way some have overlooked your music,
my desires have been seen as bag-
atelles," stuffing a forkful of pie in my mouth.
You laugh so hard I think it'll crack the window.
"*Mature* people—even mystics—
don't take themselves so seriously," you chide, spiraling

hair around your index finger. Outside, debris spirals
into a tornado—manifestation of a music
furioso. You become that wind: complaints mist

from your throat, congeal into crinkled bags.
Floating above us, they unwind
a litany of betrayals from their mouths.

"I know, I know," I mouth.
My unspoken words become bricks in a spire. *All*
of us feel unheard, unloved, I think. Then: *thwack!* Wind
thrusts open the door while the music
of Mahler keens as mournfully as bag-
pipes. The absence that enters could be the "me" you've missed.

I've become an apparition, shade of mist,
your accompaniment. As you press your mouth
to the coffee's foam, two enormous bags
wheeze into the café like asthmatic lungs. Your animus spirals
with a suppressed music,
not played . . . whined.

Winding over our table, the bags glide like mist
as the music diminuendos. The bags open their mouths,
spiral, & clamp over our heads.

Interior, Anterior

In the restaurant where I first tasted
        desire, my teeth clattered

against tines. Bossa nova spiraled
        from vinyl seraphim.

My lips carved words
        to exclude

my future. My cursive shadow
        scrawled,

narrative smudging
        the decades.

Lovers' names, plague-
        crumbled.

Now, my younger self
        enters an elevator to rise

into a skyscraper
        that doesn't yet exist.

Luminous Barge

for Michael Hébert

"*Aybair*, not *Heebert*—it's French," he said.
In Julius's Bar & one week less than legal, I fed

on men's attentions. Michael & I clung
to each other, buoyed through smoke that stung

my eyes. "You don't have to go back to Philly—your choice.
Stay in New York, *chez moi*," he said, voicing

my desire. "I live above the Jackson Hole. Be my guest
if you like burgers—they've got the biggest

& the best. Then we can go upstairs for dessert,"
he added, smiling. "Sounds great," I chirped.

We jammed the relished slabs in
our mouths, grease trickling down our chins.

Upstairs, he muttered, as if in response,
"About this bunk bed—had a roommate once . . ."

Sidestepping the past, he set
records on the turntable, hoping I'd forget,

then swooped back, his arms a cape
around me. The music, the books—the very landscape

of his apartment formed details of a world
that belonged to others. Compelled

to be of it, to drink its air,
I made mental sketches: bureau, Levalors, worn leather

chair. "Is that where you do your reading?"
I asked, padding across the room, proceeding

to look through slippery magazines on the table.
"You edit all these? I asked. "Boy, you're full

of questions," he said. "No, but they're all Condé Nast,
our parent company." I brushed my lips over the contrast

of textures between his cheek & neck—
the smell of soap on skin, of cologne on black

wool. "Listen, my little *kouros*,
some friends are making dinner for us

tomorrow night. I'm sure they'll like you."
I asked, "Are they translators, too?"

"Some, but most have their hands
occupied with the politics of publishing. And

now, I've got *my* hands occupied . . ." He leaned
& kissed my closed eyes. "Closer, Dean."

Sexual release tendered sleep: I floated
on his bed, a luminous barge, devoted

to him. Suddenly: *Goldfinger!* Shirley Bassey's shrill
voice scraped away sleep like a wooden strigil.

"4:30 a.m.! What the hell?"
I yelped. Startled, I jolted & fell

out of bed. "Oh, it's that drag queen bartender upstairs,
getting home from work. Just wait, there's

more"—Doris Day: *Once I had a secret love*
that lived within the heart of

me. All too soon my secret love . . .
shuddered through the floorboards, loud enough

for each word to arrive intact. "Don't worry," Michael
comforted, "he'll finish his drunken cycle

& the music will eventually end."
Michael eventually moved to California. I blended

my life with New York. Passing the Jackson Hole on East Sixty-Fourth,
I've been tempted to ring his buzzer. In truth,

I know he's not there, but I imagine the buzzer will activate
a memory-machine bringing back expatriated

selves—promises long erased.
A dusty July. Friends & I subway Manhattan's maze

to the Great Lawn, to view that multicolored cemetery:
The Quilt. I navigate grave-sized panels—territory

sprawling like patches of farmland seen from sky.
I guess we're lucky beauty can lie,

I think with a stifled laugh,
then glimpse a blue, appliquéd epitaph:

*Translator of French * Ami Très Cher*
Michael Hébert

Naming It

The problem is how to name it—
clinical term, slang, or symbol? Be bold or inhibit

yourself? Is it a silky, ring-necked dove on a nest of two
eggs or Plath's less romantic view?

"Four-letter words call too much attention,"
a poet friend warns. But why scorn sensation?

Can't Eros inform the name with his heady pulse?
A sprung rhythm starts to convulse

from the page: the glossy man in a magazine
or porn site I remember by face & . . . member, re-seen

in my mind till the two body parts disembody:
selves vying for identity.

At the Whitney: a wire self-portrait by Calder,
his name coiled into phallus—an alter

ego of id or *it*. As synecdoche, Olds
envisioned her father's severed penis—a bold

retelling of Cronus's tale? Her anger grew mythic.
Or was she simply calling him a prick?

Now, picture a Chelsea café: a man in white jeans.
My eye sweeps from face to "there" to glean

his magnitude. I quip, "Bet it's a sock in his denim."
My friend exhales, "No, a poem."

No Elegies for Porn Stars

for Arpad Miklos (Peter Kozma),
dead from suicide at age 45

I fell in love with you on page thirty-seven.
Shirtless, you slouched by a column,
thumbs inserted in pockets

like commas. My eye tapered
to your furred chest, to waist
& up again, meeting your goateed

grimace. As I turned the page, you shed
your jeans. A curve joined hip
to groin, seen in statues by Lysippus.

But your most prodigious gift: the satin
length of cock. I imagined
it could sing to me. The parting

photograph in the magazine
showed you reclining, unsheathed
sex rising in the foreground,

frenulum delicate as a tongue.
Your face blurred as if belonging
to a separate reality.

Later, when your flesh pulsed
on a lit screen, the naked men
you devoured & who devoured you,

moved as if swimming in a desktop-
aquarium. Each contour of sinew, each swell
advanced the narrative—pleasure,

the protagonist. I stuffed my eyes
with you till climax, then clicked off
the website. Your flesh-&-blood self

lived on in my Chelsea neighborhood.
I spotted you dining by the window
of a restaurant & gawped

as if I owned you, having craved
devoutly. On Twenty-Third Street:
a summer midnight. You peeled back

humid shadows, held
another man. I pictured you kissing
me. The last time, I ogled

you on a gay cruise, my stare meeting
your glower. I thought, *Arrogant,*
full of himself. But it was I, full

of what I expected you
to be, what I thought you owed me,
earned by years of yearning.

Turkish Man with Cinnamon Eyes

Whenever I meet with natural beauty / I know once again human life today / must and will be / changed.
—Nazim Hikmet

Crossing Queensborough Bridge, I dream
your gallery: Gaea, Arete, Aphrodite—

portraits of goddesses propped against rails.
With blazing frankincense grains, you singe

features into olive-wood slabs.
The cinnamon shading

of their faces is the cinnamon eclipse
of your eyes. You tell me

the Turks of Central Asia fed the tongues
of larks to children too timid

to speak. Those children then spoke in poems.
I recite *Human Landscapes from My Country,*

adding how I admire Hikmet &
how all poets are exiles. You declaim

"Penelope's Despair" by Ritsos, shadows
of wings tangling with her tapestry's

red & green threads, her loom
a cage she willingly reenters each night.

I say the world is text & we read it.
The world is history & we bleed it.

I say, *I'm unable to love. Love me.*
We stand above the bridge, peering down,

the East River rippling below us—
hair of a deity about to breathe.

Bronze

The Greek and Roman Galleries
The Metropolitan Museum of Art,
New York

His veined hand reaches out to you.
Encased in a verdigris husk,
this man cannot trudge
through battlefields & agoras, brothels & temples.

Encased in verdigris damask,
he no longer flees
battlefields & agoras, brothels & temples.
Gape into his sockets' sepulchers:

he no longer sees.
His carnelian eyes once glinted in torchlight.
Gaze into his sockets' sepulchers:
virgins cradled lilacs.

His eyes squinted in torchlight, watching
youths balance bowls of wine.
Virgins cradled lilacs,
chanting anapests in Eleusis.

Youths spilled wine into soil.
Now bronze entombs their voices,
decanting anapests from Eleusis.
In the moment's monument,

bronze entombs his voice.
This man cannot trudge
from our moment's monument.
His veined hand reaches out to us.

This Man, His Many Almond Thoughts Worn Away,

The Greek & Roman Galleries,
The Metropolitan Museum of Art,
New York

stretches toward the ceiling like a tree on the edge
 of a cliff.

A ragged cloth swags across his pectorals—
 fullness & phallus

exposed. His body is an abandoned palace
 of sweat,

unable to forget the striving of a clasped
 hand, the hamartia

that bothers life into art,
 seed into tree,

petals, hulls, leaves:
 debris.

His bronze hand unfists my seeing
 from the precipice

of doing,
 done.

The Naked Man

after a Greek vase painting at the
Metropolitan Museum,
New York

Was it
a crack in the
sky or the sudden wail
of a hawk that thrust the naked
man down

into
revelers, their
horses' necks garlanded
with chamomile buds? Falling toward
chaos,

he looked
up, bewildered.
A thunderclap roared, or
was it laughter? Reaching from robes,
cross-stitched:

honey-
suckle & palm-
fronds—hands bolstered the man's
body. But the revelers soon
forgot

him &
he fell, his gaze
transfixed, his muscled arms
raised—wings. Below, men & women
swilled dark

wine. Plunged
into gossip,
song, they lounged on engraved
couches. But the man, anointed
with oil,

powdered
with a mist of
blond sand, was not among
them—summoned by a shriek no one
could hear.

The Etruscan Chariot

The Greek and Roman Galleries,
The Metropolitan Museum of Art,
New York

is mathematical. Insect-clicking
        of cogs & gears activates

a calculator: subtract
        New York from Tarquinii.

Subtract now from when:
        bronze Achilles buzzes

through stratosphere, buffeted
        by zephyrs,

arriving faster than
        want. Conservators' hands

scour the tarnished
        sum. The chariot

glistens, wheels poised,
        immobile—

equal sign between past
        & future.

Colossus of Rust

—A Voyage of Growth and Discovery, *by Mike Kelley and Michael Smith, Sculpture Center, Long Island City, 2009*

Raising a torch to a mechanized cosmos,
this colossal infant salutes

burning sky. Amber spotlights
gutter. Chatoyant rust glows

into pollen. A makeshift heaven
of discarded coils, carburetors,

bedpans. A machine pumps piston-valves.
Yellow pennants swag, celebrate

a return no one can see. Curled
into itself like a fetus, an inner ear

can't hear. A boy thwacks a bronze bong:
baritone. Ancient voices

expand into air. This statue's smelted forefather
straddled Rhodes' Harbor.

His verdigris mother ushered hoards
toward Ellis Island.

But this junkyard colossus rises
        above Long Island City,

spreads diapered thighs.
        Transformed, transgendered,

he gives birth to a phantom galleon.
        On its deck, *another* infant

grasps a tablet gouged with an alphabet
        no one will speak.

The Liver Is the Cock's Comb

after a painting by Arshile Gorky

Sun-warmed apricots release their scent.
        A boy from Khorkom

breathes deep & tastes their color
        with his eyes.

War's impasto of flame.
        Charred carrion: limbs

& entrails. His famished mother
        dies in his arms. The boy draws

a scorched landscape, vermilioned.
        That artist is now

a man. He hangs his voice
        from a desiccated tear,

dusts his knees, unpeels
        his face & name.

Sails toward a new self
        in New York City.

Night blooms inside a skyscraper.
    Petals wither.

Flute-hollow skeletons exhale
    a satin sky, a coffin lining.

The painter thumbs his mother's
    embroidered apron—threads

unraveling, an Armenian prayer.
    With paint-stained hands, he bends

toward a deathbed, a flowerbed:
    every garden a cemetery.

Four

A Cannibal's Suicide

"'You must sit down,' says Love, 'and
taste my meat.' / So I did sit and eat."
—George Herbert

I stuffed my mouth with bulbs & grubs,
with locusts in wild honey—
husks crunching between my teeth.

Then a sparrow—I wanted to consume
its song. I relished the gnashing, the machinery
of jaw & incisors, transforming flesh

into vibration, filling my emptiness.
Animals foraged from midnight elms,
sniffed at my ankles:

a ferret, a muskrat, a mole.
I skinned & smeared their meat with turmeric,
with herbes de Provence. I roasted

the beasts on a spit, aromas inflaming
my nostrils. Salivating, I savored
each chew. My reputation grew

into the city. As if to mock my appetite,
larger animals offered themselves up.
How could I refuse?

I brandished my butcher knife, filleted
them, dressed their flesh for the flame.
How proficient I had become.

Had you seen me, had you smelled
the velvet smoke, you too would have smiled
as I slit a smile across the throat

of my first human.
I had nothing against him—
wanted to taste the last words he moaned

making love. Those delicious
syllables spiraled, mingling with smoke
as I wolfed his flank.

I even thanked him—a prayer.
My admiration lured another,
another . . . unbeing.

I never asked for names or reasons.
Exiles from the world sacrificed
themselves to my knife, dispensing

with formalities. These outcasts
knew I could translate their suffering
into loin, sirloin, fillet—

in balsamic glaze, in crushed black
peppercorns. As I gnawed a thigh bone,
the vapor, the songs, the spirits returned

in a braiding of shrieks.
Didn't these misfits know
I had uplifted them into art?

But the smaze twisted into a noose,
crushing my bones. I had to cut
loose—slash the fumes.

The way a matador lunges a sword
through a bull's shoulder blades
into the defiant heart, I knifed

my own. Blood pumped out—splattered
a crimson script. Dressing my meat
for another's feast, I waited to feed

myself to slavering jaws. Saliva dissolved
my flesh into pages—teeth
ground my despair into words.

Astoria

I shuttle toward singed-meat air,
toward honeyed cafés & late cigarettes.
In a church, women plant candles

in sand, ghostly flowers in a garden.
Wielders of light, let me take refuge
among flaming petals. Let forsythia

speak a waterfall of fire.
The Virgin's icon weeps
myrrh. I trace her fragrant tears.

Saint Spyridon materializes
from a mosaic. With trowel & grout,
he glues tessera to tessera, broken

glass to broken past. He points
to a catacomb maze, invites me
to follow. Descending,

we pass an electrical wire—nerve
of nameless voices, conduit between dead &
living, currents shushing.

Welder of light, teach sparks to chant
antiphonies. Teach the dead to voice
polyglot exile. Block-by-block,

build a bridge. When a brick implodes
in your hand, you proclaim
chrism, clay, fire as one entity—ash

scattering. We are spirit,
mind, meat—deceived
into permanence.

No longer formed
or deformed by desire,
I am water reciting its body.

Father Demo Square

Balancing a cupola on his head, a saint perches
above Our Lady of Pompeii, spies
on our world below. A tour bus

screeches toward Carmine Street, wheezes
chunks of smog—*GUESS*
emblazoned on its side.

A photoshopped couple in jeans dangles
from its roof like participles. No grammar
of seeing guides the sweat-

anointed tourists. Their mouths
gape like purgatory's methane caves.
Heat stuns the air.

A Wall Street broker—liberated from pinstripes—
sports an opened shirt:
tattoos, nipples pierced

with chains. When night arrives, the fountain
ignites, light puddling
in tiers. A toothless man with guitar

croons songs from the Summer of Love.
A waiter carries plates alfresco
from a trattoria. Wearing a T-shirt

with hallucinogenic script, he rants: "We all wear
the past on our backs—the first line
of the first poem."

Winter: Chumley's Courtyard

Coutured couples murmur,
shades drifting
from a vacant courtyard.
In the vibrating brilliance of streetlights,

shapes shift.
Quivering in the arch—
the vibrating brilliance of streetlights'
dimensionless glare.

Shivering in the arch,
a woman with a cart of cans & bottles.
Her dimensionless glare
grows cold as inevitability.

The woman with a cart of cans & bottles
warbles an invented language.
Wind blows cold as inevitability,
nattering to no one.

Warbling an inverted language,
she shuffles across the courtyard,
mattering to no one.
Cultured couples murmur.

Synchronicity on Twenty-First Street

Downstairs
to hurl trash in
to a sky-blue plastic
bag, I lift the lid, find grinning
false teeth

on top
of other trash
bags. So I drop the trash
& cymbal down the lid when a
man in

his late
sixties saunters
by himself: Harris tweed
suit, burgundy tie & silver
ballet

slippers
with sparkling bows.
Noticing I've noticed
him, he caterwauls to himself,
toothless.

Mad Avenue

Blown-up, black-&-white etchings of men squat
on the edge of a scaffold, advertising
PAUL STEWART.

Each giant man wears a tie three times his size:
stripes green/ocher, crimson/purple, blue/tan—
like guidons seen through 3-D glasses,

like rolled-up oriental rugs. In a 1940s road movie,
a stowaway might hide inside
one—asleep in Ohio, awakened

far away. Imagine you're there—
say, in Tahiti, or some made-up Hollywood name
like "Wahu-Wahu." Meanwhile, I'm bouncing

around in celluloid, my skin glistening with the film's
gray flickering, my blood
also gray. But now I'm in the mood

for a '50s MGM musical, with those brown-reds,
red-browns & pea-greens I find oddly appealing.
Why not dance around a Styrofoam fountain

with Cyd Charisse? Why not even *be* her? Gene Kelly
was such a catch in those days,
even if he never wore a tie.

1946

a photograph of my mother, age 16, with her mother

Flourish of breath & croon (ascent
of Big Band trumpets)
spirals five flights to your Chelsea apartment.

Smelling garlic sputter in virgin oil, seeing bracelets
swallow your wrist—hand leaning
on your mother's pale arm—I forget

decades have elapsed. Without leaping
years ahead to my birth, I recognize
your face, younger than the one seeping

from suitcased memory. The eyes
of *your* mother—toward whom I'd someday crawl
—hue of sesame, beeswax, bruise.

She wrote herself without mascara's scrawl.
Ringlets pinched into a tame
pompadour with black bows. A shawl

of crocheted cobwebs framed
her padded shoulders. Mother,
your lipstick's elegant flames

spellbound your mother, making her dress as other
than herself for the photographer. Who
was he, incorporeal as lather?

Your faces emerged from his chemical bath—its brew
buoying the myth of immigrant success.
Was he hired to make you appear well-to-do

for family in Greece? Yes,
this photograph was a talisman against despair.
You gave into beauty's sway, your tresses

storming—dark Aegean swells. Hair
eddied past your neck—a style Stanwyck or
Bacall might have worn. I stare

into your photograph, sure
I would still know you. Your eyes gaze
beneath brows' plucked allure,

past the moment where you sat—not for days
but generations—sealing me in paraphrase.

Prosopo Means Face, Mask, Person: A Memory Album of My Mother, Sofia

I

Six Years Old

You peer into the lens, bottomless
grave. Wearing a black pinafore, you clutch
a candle. A black bow alights
onto your curls. The week before, your father

had died—head heavy as a bag of plaster
on your lap. A white pigeon swooped
to the adjacent roof. Your mother named it
Parakletos.

Sixteen Years Old

You wear a pompadour & sepia
lipstick. While your eyes engage
the invisible photographer,
you force a smile, wince.

Eighteen Years Old

Your veil billows, eclipses the groom's
tuxedoed shoulder. Pearled *stéfana*

encircle your dark hair, threading your lives
together with ivory ribbons.

You pose before the Plaza Hotel fountain,
where the goddess Pomona tilts
a basket of pears that never decay. Your wedding
gown spills onto pavement like milk.

Thirty-One Years Old

You become *we*—
a family portrait posed
before our house. A bay window
frames us. If a lens peered inside,

it would see our Spanish living room:
two thrones like señoritas' combs,
credenza, wrought-iron screen.
That quixotic décor

is also your portrait. Outside,
you're squinting, but the sun
is leaden. A week before, you returned
from the mental hospital.

Thirty-Three Years Old

We're posing in front of our house again:
My brother, father, & you are a trinity—
Grandmother & I a duet, her hand
draped over my shoulder.

Your gaze is tentative—hair
softer, tousled. In a flowered dress,
you disappear behind my brother,
buttressed.

II

Sofia Portrayed by Pencil & Gouache

You wear no makeup, hair sleeked from face.
Peeling potatoes, we gouge imperfections. I complain
about my brother. Your psychiatrist's voice invades
your mouth, "That's *your* problem, not mine."

Later, you prepare for my father's
political soiree. I watch you apply makeup
from a shiny black case magicked into tiers,
mirrors. You brush bronze above your eyes,

scribe eyeliner into calligraphic points, draw
with eyebrow pencil, affix false eyelashes'
spiders. Moon dust gleams
below your brows. Unlocking

a black box, you tug its satin cord, shake
the brunette "fall" free. You tilt
your head, whoosh the glistening hair
onto your scalp. Like a magician, snapping

a cape to reveal a rabbit, you wrest the towel
from your shoulders. Your silk dress is a blur
of gouache: ocher, coral, mint. You slide a duster
from a garment bag, slip it on, mist *Je Reviens*—

step toward its beatific haze. Thrusting feet
into mint-green pumps, you grow taller,
glimpse the mirror,
plead, "Who is she?"

Rain Seen from the Gym

I park
my black gym bag
on a windowsill &
peer onto Eighth Avenue.
Trees clench

like fists
clasping dollars—
green, russet & orange.
Irrevocable descent: fall.
The plunge

into
winter will come
too soon. I want to be
a fist: clutch hours, days, months, years—
hoard this

body.
I'm here today
to build biceps, pecs, lats
(reverse gravity's distortions),
struggling

each time
to exercise
dominion over flesh.
Suddenly: fluent, yellow fire . . .
Although

I can't
see the taxi
slicing through the street—parked
cars obstructing my view—the cab's
yellow

reflects
in the puddles
between cars. It's how I
imagine spirit: scrawling flame,
unseen.

This Unexpected Clock

And your spoil shall be gathered like the gathering of the caterpillar:
as the running to and fro of locusts shall he run upon them.
—Isaiah 33:4

resists the weight of anonymity.
Embedded beneath sidewalk-glass,
sanded by frenetic years

of feet, its face leers up
like a drowned man submerged
in ice. A jewelry store window

mirrors thawing sun.
A glass façade flashes
copper. I bite

into a yellow apple, dissolve
into glare. The slogan of a long-defunct
department store wreathes the clock's face:

Buy on time
Be on time
The clock's enameled hands turn

into the scrolled I's
          of illuminated Bibles. Harp in hand, Isaiah
          chants the chirps & trills

of desert locusts. Now
          the clock hands saw with cello bows—
          tempos pulse

even as the clock slows, & time allows me,
          I imagine,
          to catch up.

Notes

This Is Not a Skyscraper alludes to Rene Magritte's surrealist masterpiece *La Trahison des images* (*Ceci n'est pas une pipe*) or *The Betrayal of Images* (*This Is Not a Pipe*).

Hermaphrodite *(page 52)*
Berdache: Plains Indian berdaches are best described as occupying an alternative or third gender role, in which traits of men and women are combined with those unique to berdache status.

Electra *(page 42)*
Varanasi: With miles of *ghats* for religious bathing, an array of shrines, temples, and palaces, this city is sacred to Hindus.

***Prosopo* Means Face, Mask, Person:** *A Memory Album of My Mother, Sofia* *(pages 121–124)*
Parakletos: Paraclete—the Holy Ghost as comforter or Advocate.
Stéfana: Wedding crowns originate in an Ancient Greek custom where the couple wore crowns made from plants devoted to Aphrodite, such as olive branches, grape leaves, & lemon blossoms.

Biographical Note

Dean Kostos's collections include *Rivering, Last Supper of the Senses, The Sentence That Ends with a Comma* (which was taught at Duke University), and the chapbook *Celestial Rust*. He co-edited *Mama's Boy: Gay Men Write about Their Mothers* (a Lambda Book Award finalist) and edited *Pomegranate Seeds: An Anthology of Greek-American Poetry* (its debut reading was held at the United Nations), and has compiled and translated poems from Ancient Greece, Byzantium, and Modern Greece for The Rockefeller Foundation Cultural Innovation Fund. His poems and personal essays have appeared in over 300 journals and anthologies, such as *The Bangalore Review* (India), *Boulevard, Chelsea, Cimarron Review, The Cincinnati Review, Mediterranean Poetry* (Sweden), *Southwest Review, Stand Magazine (UK), Stranger at Home, Token Entry, Vanitas, Western Humanities Review,* and on Oprah Winfrey's website *Oxygen.com*. His literary criticism has appeared on the Harvard UP website, in *Talisman,* and elsewhere. He has been invited to read at Harvard, Princeton, Poets House, City Lights Bookstore, and elsewhere. His choral text, *Dialogue: Angel of War, Angel of Peace,* was set to music by James Bassi and performed by Voices of Ascension, and his poem "Subway Silk" was translated into a film by Canadian filmmaker Jill Clark, shown at Tribeca and at the San Francisco IndieFest. A multiple Pushcart-Prize nominee, he has taught at Wesleyan, The Gallatin School of NYU, The City University of New York, and he has served as literary judge for Columbia University's Gold Crown Awards. A recipient of a Yaddo fellowship, he also serves on the editorial board of *Journal of the Hellenic Diaspora*. He was nominated twice for the PEN Voelcker Poetry Award.